50 Bread from Paris Recipes

By: Kelly Johnson

Table of Contents

- Baguette
- Pain de Campagne (French Country Bread)
- Pain Complet (Whole Wheat Bread)
- Focaccia
- Pain de Mie
- Pain de Poilâne (Poilâne-style Bread)
- Pain de Chef
- Brioche
- Pain Viennois
- Pain de Navarre
- Pain de Campagne au Levain (Sourdough Country Bread)
- Pain Comté
- Pain de Châtaigne (Chestnut Bread)
- Pain Complet au Levain (Sourdough Whole Wheat Bread)
- Pain de Maison (House Bread)
- Pain Pita Parisien
- Pain Boule
- Pain de Mie au Levain (Sourdough Soft Bread)
- Pain de Parisien
- Pain de Miel (Honey Bread)
- Pain de Sarrasin (Buckwheat Bread)
- Pain de Céréales (Multigrain Bread)
- Pain Complet de Sarrasin (Buckwheat Whole Wheat Bread)
- Pain d'épi (Epi-style Bread)
- Pain Parisien au Levain (Paris Sourdough Bread)
- Pain Poilâne à l'Ancienne (Old-Style Poilâne Bread)
- Pain de Maïs (Cornbread)
- Pain de Lait (Milk Bread)
- Pain de Pâques (Easter Bread)
- Pain d'Alsace
- Pain de Pain de Campagne au Levain (Sourdough Country Bread)
- Pain de Fête (Celebration Bread)
- Pain Au Levain Parisien
- Pain de Mie au Beurre (Butter Soft Bread)
- Pain Bâtard

- Pain De Toulouse
- Pain De Roti
- Pain De Pain Brioché (Brioche Bread)
- Pain Polka
- Pain de Pois Chiches (Chickpea Bread)
- Pain de Marnes
- Pain de Gruyère
- Pain Flûte
- Pain à l'Ancienne (Old-fashioned Bread)
- Pain au Levain Fermenté (Fermented Sourdough Bread)
- Pain de Trévise
- Pain de Chouette
- Pain Riche
- Pain Ail et Herbes (Garlic and Herb Bread)
- Pain d'Artichaut (Artichoke Bread)

Baguette

Ingredients:

- 500g all-purpose flour
- 350ml water
- 10g salt
- 7g active dry yeast
- 1 tablespoon olive oil
- 1 tablespoon honey

Instructions:

1. Dissolve yeast in warm water with honey and let it sit for 5-10 minutes until bubbly.
2. In a large bowl, combine flour and salt. Gradually pour in the yeast mixture and olive oil.
3. Mix until a dough forms, then knead for 10 minutes on a floured surface until smooth.
4. Place the dough in a lightly oiled bowl and cover with a damp cloth. Let it rise for 1-1.5 hours.
5. Preheat the oven to 475°F (245°C). Punch the dough down and divide it into 2 parts.
6. Shape each piece into a long baguette, place on a baking sheet lined with parchment paper.
7. Score the tops with a sharp knife and let rise for 30 minutes.
8. Bake for 20-25 minutes until golden brown. Let cool before slicing.

Pain de Campagne (French Country Bread)

Ingredients:

- 500g bread flour
- 375ml warm water
- 10g salt
- 7g active dry yeast
- 1 tablespoon sugar

Instructions:

1. In a small bowl, dissolve sugar and yeast in warm water. Let sit for 5-10 minutes until foamy.
2. Combine bread flour and salt in a large bowl, then add the yeast mixture.
3. Knead the dough on a floured surface for 10 minutes until smooth and elastic.
4. Place the dough in an oiled bowl, cover, and let rise for 1 hour or until doubled in size.
5. Punch down the dough, shape into a round loaf, and place on a baking sheet.
6. Let rise for 30-40 minutes, preheat the oven to 450°F (230°C).
7. Score the top with a knife, then bake for 25-30 minutes until golden brown.

Pain Complet (Whole Wheat Bread)

Ingredients:

- 300g whole wheat flour
- 200g all-purpose flour
- 300ml warm water
- 10g salt
- 7g active dry yeast
- 1 tablespoon honey

Instructions:

1. Dissolve yeast and honey in warm water and let it activate for 5 minutes.
2. Combine whole wheat flour, all-purpose flour, and salt in a large bowl.
3. Gradually add the yeast mixture to the flour and mix until dough forms.
4. Knead for 8-10 minutes until the dough is smooth. Place in a greased bowl and cover. Let rise for 1-1.5 hours.
5. Shape the dough into a loaf and place in a greased loaf pan. Let it rise for 30 minutes.
6. Preheat the oven to 375°F (190°C), then bake for 30-35 minutes until the top is golden.

Focaccia

Ingredients:

- 500g all-purpose flour
- 300ml warm water
- 10g salt
- 10g sugar
- 15g fresh yeast or 7g dry yeast
- 2 tablespoons olive oil
- Fresh rosemary (optional)

Instructions:

1. Dissolve the yeast and sugar in warm water, let it activate for 5-10 minutes.
2. In a large bowl, combine flour and salt, and make a well in the center.
3. Add the yeast mixture and olive oil, mix until a dough forms.
4. Knead the dough for 8-10 minutes until smooth, then place in an oiled bowl. Cover and let rise for 1 hour.
5. Preheat the oven to 400°F (200°C). Punch down the dough and press it into an oiled baking pan.
6. Use your fingers to dimple the dough, drizzle with olive oil, and sprinkle with rosemary.
7. Bake for 20-25 minutes until golden brown.

Pain de Mie

Ingredients:

- 500g bread flour
- 300ml warm milk
- 10g salt
- 7g active dry yeast
- 30g **butter**, softened
- 1 tablespoon honey

Instructions:

1. Warm the milk and dissolve the yeast and honey in it. Let it activate for 5-10 minutes.
2. In a bowl, combine bread flour and salt. Add the yeast mixture and butter, mixing until a dough forms.
3. Knead for 10 minutes, then place in an oiled bowl, cover, and let rise for 1 hour.
4. Preheat the oven to 375°F (190°C). Punch down the dough and shape it into a loaf.
5. Place the dough in a greased loaf pan and let rise for 30 minutes.
6. Bake for 30-35 minutes until golden brown and hollow when tapped.

Pain de Poilâne (Poilâne-style Bread)

Ingredients:

- 500g bread flour
- 300ml warm water
- 10g salt
- 7g active dry yeast
- 1 tablespoon honey
- 1 tablespoon olive oil

Instructions:

1. In a small bowl, dissolve honey and yeast in warm water. Let sit for 5-10 minutes.
2. Mix the flour and salt in a large bowl, then pour in the yeast mixture and olive oil.
3. Knead the dough for 10 minutes until smooth and elastic.
4. Place in an oiled bowl, cover, and let rise for 1-1.5 hours.
5. Punch down the dough, shape into a round loaf, and place on a baking sheet.
6. Let rise for another 30 minutes. Preheat the oven to 475°F (245°C).
7. Score the top of the dough and bake for 25-30 minutes until golden.

Pain de Chef

Ingredients:

- 500g all-purpose flour
- 350ml water
- 10g salt
- 7g dry yeast
- 1 tablespoon olive oil
- 1 tablespoon honey

Instructions:

1. In a bowl, mix yeast, honey, and warm water. Let sit for 10 minutes.
2. In a separate bowl, combine flour and salt. Gradually add the yeast mixture and olive oil.
3. Knead the dough for 10 minutes until smooth. Let rise in an oiled bowl for 1-1.5 hours.
4. Shape the dough into a loaf and place it on a baking sheet. Let rise for 30 minutes.
5. Preheat the oven to 450°F (230°C) and bake for 25 minutes until golden brown.

Brioche

Ingredients:

- 250g all-purpose flour
- 250g bread flour
- 200g unsalted butter, softened
- 100g sugar
- 5 large eggs
- 10g salt
- 7g active dry yeast
- 120ml milk

Instructions:

1. Activate the yeast in warm milk and let it sit for 10 minutes.
2. In a bowl, combine flour, salt, and sugar. Add the yeast mixture and eggs, and mix to form dough.
3. Gradually incorporate butter and knead for 10-15 minutes until smooth.
4. Let the dough rise in a warm place for 2 hours.
5. Punch down the dough, then shape into loaves or buns.
6. Let it rise for another hour, then bake at 350°F (175°C) for 25-30 minutes.

Pain Viennois

Ingredients:

- 500g all-purpose flour
- 300ml milk
- 30g sugar
- 10g salt
- 7g active dry yeast
- 1 tablespoon butter

Instructions:

1. Warm the milk and dissolve the yeast and sugar in it. Let sit for 10 minutes.
2. Mix the flour and salt in a large bowl. Add the yeast mixture and butter.
3. Knead the dough for 8-10 minutes, then let rise for 1 hour.
4. Shape the dough into a loaf and let rise for another 30 minutes.
5. Preheat the oven to 375°F (190°C). Bake for 25 minutes until golden brown.

Pain de Navarre (Navarre Bread)

Ingredients:

- 500g bread flour
- 300ml water
- 10g salt
- 7g active dry yeast
- 1 tablespoon honey
- 2 tablespoons olive oil

Instructions:

1. Dissolve yeast and honey in warm water. Let sit for 5-10 minutes until bubbly.
2. In a large bowl, combine bread flour and salt. Gradually add the yeast mixture and olive oil.
3. Mix to form a dough and knead for 8-10 minutes until smooth.
4. Let the dough rise in a lightly oiled bowl for 1-1.5 hours.
5. Preheat the oven to 450°F (230°C). Punch down the dough and shape it into a round or oval loaf.
6. Place the dough on a baking sheet and let rise for another 30 minutes.
7. Score the top with a sharp knife and bake for 25-30 minutes until golden brown.

Pain de Campagne au Levain (Sourdough Country Bread)

Ingredients:

- **500g bread flour**
- **200g sourdough starter**
- **300ml water**
- **10g salt**
- **1 tablespoon honey**

Instructions:

1. Mix the sourdough starter, water, and honey in a bowl.
2. Gradually add the bread flour and salt, stirring until combined.
3. Knead the dough for 10 minutes on a floured surface until smooth.
4. Let the dough rise for 1-2 hours in a warm place, or until doubled in size.
5. Shape the dough into a round loaf, and let it rise for another 1-2 hours.
6. Preheat the oven to 475°F (245°C). Score the top of the dough and bake for 30-35 minutes, until golden brown and hollow when tapped.

Pain Comté (Comté Bread)

Ingredients:

- 500g bread flour
- 300ml water
- 10g salt
- 7g active dry yeast
- 100g Comté cheese, grated
- 1 tablespoon olive oil

Instructions:

1. Dissolve yeast in warm water and let it sit for 5-10 minutes.
2. In a large bowl, combine flour and salt. Gradually add the yeast mixture and olive oil.
3. Add the grated Comté cheese and mix into the dough.
4. Knead the dough for 8-10 minutes until smooth and elastic.
5. Place in a greased bowl, cover, and let rise for 1-1.5 hours.
6. Preheat the oven to 375°F (190°C). Shape the dough into a loaf and place it on a baking sheet.
7. Let rise for 30 minutes, then bake for 25-30 minutes until golden brown.

Pain de Châtaigne (Chestnut Bread)

Ingredients:

- 400g bread flour
- 100g chestnut flour
- 300ml warm water
- 10g salt
- 7g active dry yeast
- 1 tablespoon olive oil

Instructions:

1. Dissolve the yeast in warm water and let it sit for 5-10 minutes.
2. In a large bowl, combine the bread flour, chestnut flour, and salt.
3. Gradually add the yeast mixture and olive oil, mixing until a dough forms.
4. Knead the dough for 8-10 minutes until smooth, then let it rise for 1 hour.
5. Punch down the dough, shape it into a loaf, and let it rise for another 30 minutes.
6. Preheat the oven to 400°F (200°C). Bake the bread for 25-30 minutes until golden.

Pain Complet au Levain (Sourdough Whole Wheat Bread)

Ingredients:

- 400g whole wheat flour
- 100g bread flour
- 200g sourdough starter
- 300ml warm water
- 10g salt
- 1 tablespoon honey

Instructions:

1. In a large bowl, mix the sourdough starter, water, and honey.
2. Gradually add the whole wheat flour, bread flour, and salt.
3. Knead the dough for 10-15 minutes until smooth and elastic.
4. Let the dough rise for 2-3 hours, or until doubled in size.
5. Punch down the dough, shape it into a round loaf, and let it rise for another hour.
6. Preheat the oven to 475°F (245°C). Score the top of the dough and bake for 30-35 minutes.

Pain de Maison (House Bread)

Ingredients:

- 500g all-purpose flour
- 300ml warm water
- 10g salt
- 7g active dry yeast
- 1 tablespoon olive oil
- 1 tablespoon honey

Instructions:

1. Dissolve yeast and honey in warm water, and let it activate for 10 minutes.
2. Mix flour and salt in a bowl, then add the yeast mixture and olive oil.
3. Knead the dough for 8-10 minutes on a floured surface until smooth.
4. Let the dough rise in an oiled bowl for 1-1.5 hours.
5. Preheat the oven to 375°F (190°C). Punch down the dough, shape it into a loaf, and place it on a baking sheet.
6. Let the dough rise for 30 minutes, then bake for 25-30 minutes until golden brown.

Pain Pita Parisien (Parisian Pita Bread)

Ingredients:

- 500g bread flour
- 300ml warm water
- 10g salt
- 7g active dry yeast
- 1 tablespoon olive oil

Instructions:

1. Dissolve yeast in warm water and let it sit for 5-10 minutes.
2. Mix flour and salt in a bowl, then add the yeast mixture and olive oil.
3. Knead the dough for 8-10 minutes until smooth, then let rise for 1 hour.
4. Preheat the oven to 450°F (230°C). Divide the dough into small balls and roll them into flat circles.
5. Place the pita dough onto a baking sheet and bake for 5-7 minutes, until puffed and lightly browned.

Pain Boule (Round Bread)

Ingredients:

- 500g bread flour
- 300ml warm water
- 10g salt
- 7g active dry yeast
- 1 tablespoon olive oil

Instructions:

1. Dissolve yeast in warm water and let it sit for 5-10 minutes.
2. Combine flour and salt in a bowl. Gradually add the yeast mixture and olive oil.
3. Knead for 10 minutes, then let rise in a greased bowl for 1-1.5 hours.
4. Punch down the dough, shape into a round boule, and let it rise for another 30-40 minutes.
5. Preheat the oven to 475°F (245°C). Score the top of the dough and bake for 25-30 minutes.

Pain de Mie au Levain (Sourdough Soft Bread)

Ingredients:

- **500g bread flour**
- **200g sourdough starter**
- **300ml warm water**
- **10g salt**
- **1 tablespoon honey**

Instructions:

1. Mix the sourdough starter, warm water, and honey in a bowl.
2. Gradually add the flour and salt to form a dough.
3. Knead the dough for 10-15 minutes, then place it in a greased bowl to rise for 1-2 hours.
4. Punch down the dough and shape it into a loaf, then let it rise for another hour.
5. Preheat the oven to 375°F (190°C). Score the top of the dough and bake for 30-35 minutes.

Pain de Parisien (Parisian Bread)

Ingredients:

- **500g all-purpose flour**
- **300ml water**
- **10g salt**
- **7g active dry yeast**
- **1 tablespoon olive oil**

Instructions:

1. Dissolve yeast in warm water, and let it activate for 10 minutes.
2. In a large bowl, combine flour and salt. Gradually add the yeast mixture and olive oil.
3. Knead the dough for 10 minutes until smooth, then let rise for 1 hour.
4. Preheat the oven to 450°F (230°C). Shape the dough into a loaf and place it on a baking sheet.
5. Let the dough rise for 30 minutes, then score the top and bake for 25-30 minutes until golden brown.

Pain de Miel (Honey Bread)

Ingredients:

- 500g bread flour
- 300ml warm water
- 10g salt
- 7g active dry yeast
- 2 tablespoons honey
- 1 tablespoon olive oil

Instructions:

1. Dissolve the yeast and honey in warm water and let it activate for 5-10 minutes.
2. In a large bowl, combine the flour and salt. Gradually add the yeast mixture and olive oil.
3. Mix until combined, then knead the dough for 8-10 minutes until smooth and elastic.
4. Cover the dough with a clean towel and let it rise for 1-1.5 hours, or until doubled in size.
5. Preheat the oven to 375°F (190°C). Punch down the dough and shape it into a loaf.
6. Place the dough on a baking sheet, and let it rise for 30 minutes.
7. Bake for 25-30 minutes until the bread is golden brown and sounds hollow when tapped on the bottom.

Pain de Sarrasin (Buckwheat Bread)

Ingredients:

- 300g buckwheat flour
- 200g bread flour
- 300ml warm water
- 10g salt
- 7g active dry yeast
- 1 tablespoon olive oil

Instructions:

1. In a bowl, dissolve the yeast in warm water and let it sit for 5-10 minutes.
2. In a separate large bowl, combine the buckwheat flour, bread flour, and salt.
3. Gradually add the yeast mixture and olive oil, stirring until combined.
4. Knead the dough for 8-10 minutes until smooth and slightly sticky.
5. Let the dough rise in a lightly oiled bowl for 1-1.5 hours.
6. Preheat the oven to 400°F (200°C). Punch down the dough and shape it into a loaf.
7. Place the dough on a baking sheet, cover, and let rise for 30-45 minutes.
8. Bake for 25-30 minutes until the bread is golden and sounds hollow when tapped.

Pain de Céréales (Multigrain Bread)

Ingredients:

- 300g bread flour
- 100g rolled oats
- 50g sunflower seeds
- 50g flaxseeds
- 300ml warm water
- 10g salt
- 7g active dry yeast
- 2 tablespoons honey

Instructions:

1. Dissolve the yeast and honey in warm water and let it sit for 5-10 minutes.
2. In a large bowl, combine the bread flour, oats, sunflower seeds, flaxseeds, and salt.
3. Gradually add the yeast mixture and stir until combined.
4. Knead the dough for 8-10 minutes until smooth and elastic.
5. Cover the dough and let it rise in a warm place for 1-1.5 hours.
6. Preheat the oven to 375°F (190°C). Punch down the dough and shape it into a loaf.
7. Let the dough rise for another 30 minutes, then bake for 30-35 minutes until golden brown.

Pain Complet de Sarrasin (Buckwheat Whole Wheat Bread)

Ingredients:

- 300g buckwheat flour
- 200g whole wheat flour
- 300ml warm water
- 10g salt
- 7g active dry yeast
- 1 tablespoon olive oil

Instructions:

1. Dissolve the yeast in warm water and let it activate for 5-10 minutes.
2. In a large bowl, combine the buckwheat flour, whole wheat flour, and salt.
3. Add the yeast mixture and olive oil, and mix until a dough forms.
4. Knead the dough for 8-10 minutes until smooth and slightly sticky.
5. Let the dough rise in an oiled bowl for 1-1.5 hours.
6. Preheat the oven to 400°F (200°C). Punch down the dough and shape it into a loaf.
7. Let it rise for another 30 minutes, then bake for 30-35 minutes until golden.

Pain d'épi (Epi-style Bread)

Ingredients:

- **500g bread flour**
- **300ml warm water**
- **10g salt**
- **7g active dry yeast**
- **1 tablespoon olive oil**
- **1 tablespoon honey**

Instructions:

1. Dissolve yeast and honey in warm water and let sit for 5-10 minutes.
2. In a large bowl, combine flour and salt. Gradually add the yeast mixture and olive oil.
3. Knead the dough for 8-10 minutes until smooth and elastic.
4. Let the dough rise for 1-1.5 hours, or until doubled in size.
5. Punch down the dough and shape it into a long baguette-style loaf.
6. Use a sharp knife to cut the loaf into a wheat sheaf-like shape.
7. Let the dough rise for 30 minutes, then bake at 375°F (190°C) for 25-30 minutes until golden brown.

Pain Parisien au Levain (Paris Sourdough Bread)

Ingredients:

- **500g bread flour**
- **200g sourdough starter**
- **300ml warm water**
- **10g salt**
- **1 tablespoon honey**

Instructions:

1. Mix the sourdough starter, water, and honey in a bowl.
2. Gradually add the bread flour and salt, stirring until a dough forms.
3. Knead for 10 minutes until smooth and elastic.
4. Let the dough rise in a warm place for 2-3 hours.
5. Punch down the dough, shape it into a round loaf, and let it rise for another hour.
6. Preheat the oven to 475°F (245°C). Bake the loaf for 25-30 minutes, until golden brown.

Pain Poilâne à l'Ancienne (Old-Style Poilâne Bread)

Ingredients:

- 500g bread flour
- 100g whole wheat flour
- 300ml warm water
- 10g salt
- 7g active dry yeast
- 1 tablespoon olive oil

Instructions:

1. Dissolve yeast in warm water and let it sit for 5-10 minutes.
2. In a large bowl, combine the bread flour, whole wheat flour, and salt.
3. Add the yeast mixture and olive oil, and knead the dough for 10 minutes.
4. Let the dough rise for 1-1.5 hours, or until doubled in size.
5. Punch down the dough, shape it into a round loaf, and let it rise for another hour.
6. Preheat the oven to 450°F (230°C). Bake for 30-35 minutes until golden brown.

Pain de Maïs (Cornbread)

Ingredients:

- 300g cornmeal
- 200g all-purpose flour
- 200ml milk
- 10g salt
- 7g active dry yeast
- 2 eggs
- 2 tablespoons honey

Instructions:

1. Dissolve the yeast in warm milk and let it activate for 5-10 minutes.
2. In a large bowl, combine cornmeal, flour, and salt.
3. Add the activated yeast mixture, eggs, and honey. Stir until well combined.
4. Knead the dough for 5-8 minutes until smooth.
5. Let the dough rise for 1 hour, then shape it into a loaf.
6. Preheat the oven to 375°F (190°C). Bake for 25-30 minutes until golden and firm.

Pain de Lait (Milk Bread)

Ingredients:

- **500g bread flour**
- **250ml milk**
- **10g salt**
- **7g active dry yeast**
- **1 tablespoon sugar**
- **2 tablespoons butter**

Instructions:

1. Warm the milk slightly and dissolve the sugar and yeast in it. Let sit for 5-10 minutes.
2. In a large bowl, combine bread flour and salt. Gradually add the yeast mixture and melted butter.
3. Stir until combined, then knead the dough for 8-10 minutes until smooth and elastic.
4. Let the dough rise in an oiled bowl for 1-1.5 hours.
5. Preheat the oven to 375°F (190°C). Punch down the dough and shape it into a loaf.
6. Let it rise for another 30 minutes, then bake for 25-30 minutes until golden brown.

Pain de Pâques (Easter Bread)

Ingredients:

- 500g bread flour
- 300ml warm water
- 10g salt
- 7g active dry yeast
- 2 tablespoons sugar
- 3 eggs
- 1 teaspoon vanilla extract
- 100g melted butter
- Zest of 1 lemon
- 1 egg (for glazing)

Instructions:

1. In a bowl, dissolve the yeast and sugar in warm water. Let it activate for 5-10 minutes.
2. In a separate bowl, whisk together the flour and salt. Add the yeast mixture, eggs, vanilla, melted butter, and lemon zest.
3. Mix until combined, then knead for 8-10 minutes until smooth and elastic.
4. Let the dough rise in an oiled bowl for 1.5 hours, or until doubled in size.
5. Preheat the oven to 350°F (175°C). Punch down the dough, shape it into a round loaf or braid, and place it on a baking sheet.
6. Let it rise for another 30-45 minutes. Brush the loaf with beaten egg.
7. Bake for 30-35 minutes until golden brown.

Pain d'Alsace

Ingredients:

- **500g bread flour**
- **300ml warm water**
- **10g salt**
- **7g active dry yeast**
- **2 tablespoons olive oil**
- **1 tablespoon sugar**
- **100g diced bacon or lardons (optional)**

Instructions:

1. Dissolve the yeast and sugar in warm water and let it sit for 5-10 minutes.
2. In a large bowl, combine the flour and salt. Gradually add the yeast mixture and olive oil.
3. Knead the dough for 8-10 minutes until smooth and elastic. If using bacon, fold it into the dough after kneading.
4. Let the dough rise in a warm place for 1-1.5 hours.
5. Preheat the oven to 375°F (190°C). Punch down the dough and shape it into a round loaf or baguette.
6. Let it rise for 30 minutes, then bake for 25-30 minutes until golden and hollow when tapped.

Pain de Campagne au Levain (Sourdough Country Bread)

Ingredients:

- 500g bread flour
- 200g sourdough starter
- 300ml warm water
- 10g salt
- 1 tablespoon olive oil

Instructions:

1. Mix the sourdough starter, warm water, and olive oil in a bowl.
2. Gradually add the bread flour and salt, mixing until a dough forms.
3. Knead the dough for 10 minutes until smooth and elastic.
4. Let the dough rise in an oiled bowl for 2-3 hours, or until doubled in size.
5. Punch down the dough and shape it into a round loaf. Let it rise for another hour.
6. Preheat the oven to 475°F (245°C). Place the dough on a baking sheet or Dutch oven.
7. Bake for 30-35 minutes until golden and sounds hollow when tapped.

Pain de Fête (Celebration Bread)

Ingredients:

- **500g bread flour**
- **300ml warm water**
- **10g salt**
- **7g active dry yeast**
- **2 tablespoons honey**
- **100g dried fruits (raisins, apricots, etc.)**
- **1 egg (for glazing)**

Instructions:

1. Dissolve the yeast and honey in warm water and let it activate for 5-10 minutes.
2. In a large bowl, combine the flour and salt. Gradually add the yeast mixture.
3. Knead the dough for 8-10 minutes, then fold in the dried fruits.
4. Let the dough rise in a warm place for 1-1.5 hours.
5. Preheat the oven to 350°F (175°C). Punch down the dough and shape it into a festive loaf or wreath.
6. Let it rise for another 30 minutes, then glaze with beaten egg.
7. Bake for 30-35 minutes until golden brown.

Pain Au Levain Parisien (Parisian Sourdough Bread)

Ingredients:

- 500g bread flour
- 200g sourdough starter
- 300ml warm water
- 10g salt
- 1 tablespoon honey

Instructions:

1. Combine the sourdough starter, warm water, and honey in a bowl.
2. Gradually add the bread flour and salt, mixing until a dough forms.
3. Knead the dough for 10 minutes until smooth.
4. Let the dough rise in a warm place for 2-3 hours.
5. Shape the dough into a round or oval loaf, and let it rise for another hour.
6. Preheat the oven to 475°F (245°C). Bake the loaf for 30-35 minutes, until golden and hollow when tapped.

Pain de Mie au Beurre (Butter Soft Bread)

Ingredients:

- **500g bread flour**
- **300ml warm milk**
- **10g salt**
- **7g active dry yeast**
- **100g unsalted butter, softened**
- **1 tablespoon sugar**

Instructions:

1. Dissolve the yeast and sugar in warm milk and let it sit for 5-10 minutes.
2. In a large bowl, combine the flour and salt. Gradually add the yeast mixture and softened butter.
3. Knead the dough for 10 minutes until smooth and elastic.
4. Let the dough rise in a warm place for 1.5 hours.
5. Preheat the oven to 350°F (175°C). Punch down the dough and shape it into a loaf.
6. Let it rise for another 30 minutes, then bake for 30-35 minutes until golden brown.

Pain Bâtard

Ingredients:

- 500g bread flour
- 300ml warm water
- 10g salt
- 7g active dry yeast
- 2 tablespoons olive oil

Instructions:

1. Dissolve the yeast in warm water and let it activate for 5-10 minutes.
2. In a bowl, combine the flour and salt. Gradually add the yeast mixture and olive oil.
3. Knead the dough for 8-10 minutes until smooth.
4. Let the dough rise for 1-1.5 hours.
5. Punch down the dough, shape it into a bâtard loaf, and let it rise for another hour.
6. Preheat the oven to 400°F (200°C). Bake for 25-30 minutes, until golden and hollow when tapped.

Pain De Toulouse

Ingredients:

- **500g bread flour**
- **300ml warm water**
- **10g salt**
- **7g active dry yeast**
- **2 tablespoons olive oil**
- **1 tablespoon honey**

Instructions:

1. Dissolve the yeast and honey in warm water and let it activate for 5-10 minutes.
2. In a large bowl, combine the flour and salt. Gradually add the yeast mixture and olive oil.
3. Knead the dough for 8-10 minutes until smooth.
4. Let the dough rise for 1-1.5 hours.
5. Punch down the dough and shape it into a round loaf. Let it rise for another 30 minutes.
6. Preheat the oven to 375°F (190°C). Bake for 25-30 minutes, until golden brown.

Pain De Roti

Ingredients:

- 500g bread flour
- 300ml warm water
- 10g salt
- 7g active dry yeast
- 2 tablespoons olive oil
- 1 tablespoon sugar

Instructions:

1. Dissolve the yeast and sugar in warm water and let it activate for 5-10 minutes.
2. In a large bowl, combine the flour and salt. Gradually add the yeast mixture and olive oil.
3. Knead the dough for 8-10 minutes until smooth.
4. Let the dough rise for 1.5 hours.
5. Shape the dough into a round loaf, and let it rise for another 30 minutes.
6. Preheat the oven to 375°F (190°C). Bake for 25-30 minutes until golden brown.

Pain De Pain Brioché (Brioche Bread)

Ingredients:

- 500g bread flour
- 300g butter, softened
- 100g sugar
- 6 large eggs
- 200ml milk
- 10g salt
- 7g active dry yeast

Instructions:

1. In a small bowl, dissolve the yeast in warm milk and let it sit for 5-10 minutes.
2. In a large mixing bowl, combine the flour, sugar, and salt. Make a well in the center.
3. Add the yeast mixture and eggs into the well, and mix until the dough comes together.
4. Knead the dough for 10-12 minutes, until smooth and elastic.
5. Gradually add in the softened butter, a little at a time, continuing to knead until fully incorporated.
6. Cover the dough and let it rise for 2-3 hours, or until doubled in size.
7. Punch down the dough and shape it into a loaf. Let it rise again for 1-2 hours.
8. Preheat the oven to 375°F (190°C). Brush the top of the dough with egg wash (1 egg beaten with 1 tablespoon water).
9. Bake for 30-35 minutes until golden brown and hollow when tapped.

Pain Polka

Ingredients:

- 500g bread flour
- 300ml warm water
- 10g salt
- 7g active dry yeast
- 1 tablespoon olive oil
- 1 tablespoon sugar
- 2 teaspoons mixed herbs (optional)

Instructions:

1. Dissolve the yeast and sugar in warm water and let it activate for 5-10 minutes.
2. In a large mixing bowl, combine the flour and salt. Gradually add the yeast mixture and olive oil.
3. Mix and knead for 10 minutes, until the dough becomes smooth and elastic.
4. Let the dough rise in an oiled bowl for 1.5-2 hours, until doubled in size.
5. Punch down the dough, shape it into a round or oval loaf, and let it rise for another hour.
6. Preheat the oven to 400°F (200°C). Bake the bread for 25-30 minutes, until golden and hollow when tapped.
7. Optional: Sprinkle mixed herbs on top before baking for an extra flavor boost.

Pain de Pois Chiches (Chickpea Bread)

Ingredients:

- 400g chickpea flour
- 100g bread flour
- 300ml warm water
- 10g salt
- 7g active dry yeast
- 1 tablespoon olive oil
- 1 tablespoon honey (optional)

Instructions:

1. In a small bowl, dissolve the yeast and honey in warm water, and let it sit for 5-10 minutes.
2. In a larger bowl, mix the chickpea flour and bread flour together. Add the salt.
3. Gradually add the yeast mixture to the flour and stir until combined.
4. Knead the dough for about 8-10 minutes until it becomes smooth and elastic.
5. Let the dough rise for 1.5-2 hours until doubled in size.
6. Shape the dough into a round or oval loaf and place it on a greased baking sheet.
7. Let it rise for another 45 minutes, then preheat the oven to 375°F (190°C).
8. Bake for 30-35 minutes, until golden and firm to the touch.

Pain de Marnes

Ingredients:

- 500g bread flour
- 300ml warm water
- 10g salt
- 7g active dry yeast
- 1 tablespoon sugar
- 2 tablespoons olive oil
- 1 tablespoon sesame seeds (optional)

Instructions:

1. Dissolve the yeast and sugar in warm water, and let it sit for 5-10 minutes.
2. Combine the flour and salt in a large bowl. Gradually add the yeast mixture and olive oil.
3. Mix until the dough comes together, then knead for 10 minutes until smooth.
4. Let the dough rise in a warm place for 1-1.5 hours, or until doubled in size.
5. Punch down the dough and shape it into a loaf. Optionally, sprinkle sesame seeds on top.
6. Let the dough rise for another 30-45 minutes.
7. Preheat the oven to 375°F (190°C) and bake the bread for 30-35 minutes until golden brown and hollow when tapped.

Pain de Gruyère

Ingredients:

- 500g bread flour
- 300ml warm water
- 10g salt
- 7g active dry yeast
- 200g Gruyère cheese, grated
- 1 tablespoon olive oil
- 1 teaspoon mustard (optional)

Instructions:

1. In a bowl, dissolve the yeast in warm water and let it sit for 5-10 minutes.
2. In a large bowl, combine the flour and salt. Add the yeast mixture and olive oil.
3. Knead the dough for 10 minutes until smooth. Gradually fold in the grated Gruyère cheese.
4. Let the dough rise in a warm place for 1-1.5 hours, until doubled.
5. Punch down the dough and shape it into a loaf. Let it rise for another hour.
6. Preheat the oven to 375°F (190°C). Bake for 30-35 minutes until golden and the cheese has melted into the bread.

Pain Flûte

Ingredients:

- 500g bread flour
- 300ml warm water
- 10g salt
- 7g active dry yeast
- 2 tablespoons olive oil

Instructions:

1. Dissolve the yeast in warm water and let it sit for 5-10 minutes.
2. Combine the flour and salt in a large bowl. Gradually add the yeast mixture and olive oil.
3. Knead the dough for 10 minutes until smooth and elastic.
4. Let the dough rise for 1.5 hours, or until doubled in size.
5. Punch down the dough and shape it into a long, thin baguette-like loaf.
6. Let the dough rise for another hour. Preheat the oven to 400°F (200°C).
7. Bake the bread for 25-30 minutes until golden brown and hollow when tapped.

Pain à l'Ancienne (Old-fashioned Bread)

Ingredients:

- 500g bread flour
- 300ml warm water
- 10g salt
- 7g active dry yeast
- 1 tablespoon honey
- 2 tablespoons olive oil

Instructions:

1. Dissolve the yeast and honey in warm water, and let it sit for 5-10 minutes.
2. In a large bowl, combine the flour and salt. Gradually add the yeast mixture and olive oil.
3. Knead the dough for about 10 minutes until smooth and elastic.
4. Let the dough rise in a warm place for 1.5-2 hours, until doubled.
5. Punch down the dough and shape it into a round or oval loaf. Let it rise for another 30 minutes.
6. Preheat the oven to 375°F (190°C). Bake for 30-35 minutes until golden brown and sounds hollow when tapped.

Pain au Levain Fermenté (Fermented Sourdough Bread)

Ingredients:

- **500g bread flour**
- **200g sourdough starter (active)**
- **300ml warm water**
- **10g salt**
- **1 tablespoon honey (optional)**

Instructions:

1. In a large bowl, combine the bread flour, sourdough starter, and warm water. Stir until the dough forms.
2. Add the salt and honey (if using), then knead the dough for 10-15 minutes until smooth and elastic.
3. Place the dough in an oiled bowl and cover it with a cloth. Let it rise for 4-6 hours, or until doubled in size.
4. Punch down the dough and shape it into a round or oval loaf. Place it on a parchment-lined baking sheet or in a proofing basket.
5. Let the dough rise again for 1-2 hours until it has doubled in size.
6. Preheat the oven to 450°F (230°C). Place a shallow pan of water in the oven to create steam.
7. Score the top of the dough with a sharp knife or razor blade, then bake for 30-40 minutes until golden brown and hollow when tapped.

Pain de Trévise

Ingredients:

- **500g bread flour**
- **10g salt**
- **7g active dry yeast**
- **300ml warm water**
- **2 tablespoons olive oil**
- **1 tablespoon honey (optional)**

Instructions:

1. Dissolve the yeast and honey in warm water, and let it activate for 5-10 minutes.
2. In a large bowl, mix the flour and salt. Gradually add the yeast mixture and olive oil.
3. Knead the dough for 10 minutes until smooth and elastic.
4. Place the dough in an oiled bowl, cover with a cloth, and let it rise for 1.5-2 hours, or until doubled in size.
5. Punch down the dough, shape it into a round loaf, and let it rise for another 45 minutes.
6. Preheat the oven to 375°F (190°C). Bake for 30-35 minutes until golden and hollow when tapped.

Pain de Chouette

Ingredients:

- 500g bread flour
- 7g active dry yeast
- 300ml warm water
- 10g salt
- 2 tablespoons olive oil
- 1 tablespoon sugar (optional)

Instructions:

1. Dissolve the yeast and sugar (if using) in warm water and let it activate for 5-10 minutes.
2. In a large mixing bowl, combine the flour and salt. Add the yeast mixture and olive oil, mixing to form a dough.
3. Knead for 8-10 minutes until the dough is smooth and elastic.
4. Let the dough rise in an oiled bowl, covered with a cloth, for 1-1.5 hours until doubled in size.
5. Punch down the dough and shape it into a round or oval loaf. Let it rise for another 30-45 minutes.
6. Preheat the oven to 375°F (190°C). Bake for 25-30 minutes until golden brown and hollow when tapped.

Pain Riche (Rich Bread)

Ingredients:

- 500g bread flour
- 100g sugar
- 10g salt
- 1 tablespoon butter, softened
- 300ml warm milk
- 7g active dry yeast
- 3 large eggs

Instructions:

1. In a small bowl, dissolve the yeast in warm milk and let it sit for 5-10 minutes.
2. In a large mixing bowl, combine the flour, sugar, and salt. Add the yeast mixture, butter, and eggs.
3. Mix and knead for 10-12 minutes until the dough is smooth and elastic.
4. Let the dough rise for 2-3 hours, or until doubled in size.
5. Punch down the dough and shape it into a loaf. Let it rise again for 45 minutes.
6. Preheat the oven to 375°F (190°C). Bake the bread for 30-35 minutes until golden and sounds hollow when tapped.

Pain Ail et Herbes (Garlic and Herb Bread)

Ingredients:

- 500g bread flour
- 10g salt
- 7g active dry yeast
- 300ml warm water
- 3 tablespoons olive oil
- 4 cloves garlic, minced
- 2 teaspoons mixed dried herbs (e.g., rosemary, thyme, oregano)

Instructions:

1. In a small bowl, dissolve the yeast in warm water and let it activate for 5-10 minutes.
2. In a large bowl, combine the flour, salt, garlic, and mixed herbs. Gradually add the yeast mixture and olive oil.
3. Knead the dough for 8-10 minutes until smooth and elastic.
4. Let the dough rise in a covered bowl for 1-1.5 hours, or until doubled in size.
5. Punch down the dough and shape it into a loaf. Let it rise for another 45 minutes.
6. Preheat the oven to 375°F (190°C). Bake for 30-35 minutes until golden and fragrant.

Pain d'Artichaut (Artichoke Bread)

Ingredients:

- **500g bread flour**
- **10g salt**
- **7g active dry yeast**
- **300ml warm water**
- **1 can (400g) artichoke hearts, drained and chopped**
- **1 tablespoon olive oil**
- **1 teaspoon dried rosemary (optional)**

Instructions:

1. Dissolve the yeast in warm water and let it sit for 5-10 minutes.
2. In a large bowl, combine the flour and salt. Add the yeast mixture and olive oil, mixing to form a dough.
3. Knead the dough for 8-10 minutes until smooth. Incorporate the chopped artichokes and rosemary (if using).
4. Let the dough rise for 1.5-2 hours until doubled in size.
5. Punch down the dough, shape it into a loaf, and let it rise for another 45 minutes.
6. Preheat the oven to 375°F (190°C). Bake for 30-35 minutes until golden and hollow when tapped.

www.ingramcontent.com/pod-product-compliance
Lightning Source LLC
LaVergne TN
LVHW081332060526
838201LV00055B/2589